W. W. GOODPASTURE, EDITOR

chapter on rose hobbies, including simple directions showing how you can actually develop your
own plants and create your own varieties. Clear,
how-to-do-it illustrations supplement the text. With
the help of this book, you can surround your home
with fragrant, lovely roses, the most popular of
flowers. The author says: "My mother often said

(see back end paper)

Roses

Rinehart's Garden Library

W. W. GOODPASTURE, GENERAL EDITOR

Already Published:

Evergreens	*L. L. Kumlien*
Small Fruits	*Ralph E. Barker*
Vegetables	*Jack M. Swartout*
Annuals	*Ann Roe Robbins*
Roses	*Roy E. Shepherd*
Lawns	*John D. Bernard*

Watch for these titles:

House Plants

Shade Trees

Perennials

Soil Conditioning

Fruit Trees

Exhibiting

Bulbs

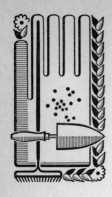

ROSES

Roy E. Shepherd

author of History of the Rose

illustrated by Rebecca and Douglas Merrilees

Rinehart & Company, Inc.

232 Madison Ave.

New York 16, N. Y.

103 St. Clair Ave., West

Toronto 5, Canada

Contents

826859

chapter one

Why you should

grow roses

The theme of this chapter comes from one who has grown roses for many years, has become imbued with a love for them and is convinced that their culture is not difficult if a few basic rules are followed. The opinion that rose growing is a highly specialized phase of gardening, requiring a tremendous amount of labor, expense and experience is erroneous and far too prevalent. Admittedly, their culture is a bit more complicated than that of some other plants, but are not the infinitely more beautiful results worth the slight additional effort?

No other flower can possibly give greater enjoyment and a garden without roses seemingly lacks distinction. Surely it is a flower which stands alone, apart from and distinguished from all others.

Rose growing, like other worth-while endeavors, presents certain problems, none of which are insurmountable, and they both challenge and intrigue the genuine gardener. If love for the rose is lacking at the outset of his endeavors, it will soon be instilled and his objective will become not "how to grow roses," but "how to grow better roses." The compensation is surely greater than the effort required.

Cultural recommendations have changed so frequently and radically during recent years that the would-be and should-be rose grower is understandably rose-shy, confused and fearful that he will not succeed. That most of these greatly differing recommendations have given success should be proof that roses will tolerate and thrive under various conditions. In fact, a love of roses plus the application of a reasonable amount of common sense and effort are the prime requisites in successful rose culture. It is often surprising to see how much abuse a rose plant will take, and if there were only one way to grow them, they would lose much of their interest.

The rose is a versatile, rugged plant with an inherent desire to live and will thrive under conditions that some writers have considered exceedingly unfavorable. Successful culture may be assured by following the few sound, but flexible, rules that follow in subsequent chapters. If the basic fundamentals of good plants, ample soil preparation, proper fertilization, precautionary measures against disease and pests, suitable winter protection and intelligent pruning are known, much can be learned by practical thinking and by trial.

Modern chemistry has overcome practically all the hazards of disease and pests; balanced fertilizers that are clean and easy to handle produce remarkable results, and rare is the soil or region in which roses cannot be grown.

There is a rose for nearly every gardening purpose. Whether you own your own home or not, you owe it to yourself and your family to enjoy Nature's most beautiful, enchanting, romantic and adaptable creation, the rose.

The growing of roses comes nearer to having universal appeal than any other avocation. It deserves this distinction because it is not only one of the least expensive of all hobbies, but offers release from worldly problems, and gives the grower both healthful exercise and an increased appreciation of Nature's beauty. Add the growing of roses to your daily routine and you will realize why the rose has been referred to as the "Queen of Flowers" for over two thousand years. You will not only enjoy it, but you will benefit physically, mentally and probably economically.

Roses will invariably widen one's social contacts, as a rose garden is the privilege of the small-lot owner as well as that of the owner of a large country estate. All homeowners agree that a house is not a home until the grounds are landscaped, and there is no better subject than the rose.

Eventually, the average rose grower will probably attempt to propagate his own plants, do a bit of breeding or exhibit his blooms in a local rose or flower show. All of these ventures add zest to the growing of roses, and the first success in any of them will be a long-remembered event.

Some who contemplate the planting of a rose garden

may feel that the initial cost is too great, but it should be borne in mind that the cost is really spread over a period of years. Actually, roses are less costly than most other plants as the life expectancy is high (several in my garden are over twenty-five years old), and the cost per blossom over a long period is remarkably low. The garden budget should be the deciding factor as to the number planted. Lack of ambition should not deter you from growing roses, as they require less time than many perennial or annual flowers, and none offer more enjoyment.

Roses are a diversified group of plants, and there are types for a variety of purposes. Some are at home in formal, informal, naturalistic or foundation plantings. Others may be used for hedges, ground covers, to break the monotony of a wall or fence, or to train on arches and pillars as accent points. Varieties and types for specific uses will be discussed later.

When we consider the adaptability of the rose and the long season of bloom as compared to that of other flowering plants, we fuller appreciate its value. Plant a few this year and you will marvel at the pleasure they will give you and their ease of culture.

✳✳✳✳✳✳✳✳✳✳

For the Rose Doth Deserve the Chiefest
Place Among All Flowers Whatsoever.
                    Gerards Herballe, 1633

chapter two

Soils and nutrient

requirements

The soil in your garden is vitally important and may determine whether your gardening endeavors are successful or not. Rarely is its quality an inducement to buy a home, and it is often necessary to replace it with good soil or to improve it by spading in adequate amounts of organic materials.

The amount required depends upon the basic soil type but from 5 to 10 per cent, by volume, of cow manure, humus (partially decomposed organic matter), peat moss or other organic materials will usually suffice. It is even possible to improve the physical structure of pure sand or heavy clay subsoil from basement excavations to such a degree that it will support quite satisfactory plant growth. In extreme cases, however, as much as 20 or 30 per cent of organic materials may be required.

It is impossible to make precise soil recommendations without a knowledge of existing conditions; but generally speaking soil that will grow good grass, flowers of variety, vegetables or even strong, healthy weeds will come close to satisfying the requirements of roses. Poor soil must be conditioned before it will support growth successfully, and even good soil requires seasonal attention and replacement.

Roses are reasonably tolerant in their requirements; but soil, to be fully productive, must be sufficiently well aerated and moisture retentive and possess, in an available form and in proper proportion, the mineral nutrients required for normal plant development. Adequate amounts of organic matter in the soil will encourage a free movement of air and water, increase the water-holding capacity of the soil, improve drainage, provide food for beneficial soil bacteria and, as in decomposing, supply certain nutrients.

A compost pile where garden refuse and other waste vegetation can be decomposed is a valuable adjunct to any garden. If properly prepared, such a pile usually contains all the essentials for plant growth. Your State Agricultural College or Experiment Station probably has bulletins on this subject.

The acidity or alkalinity of the soil should not greatly concern the rose grower if he maintains soil fertility, as very fine roses can be grown on soils that vary considerably in this respect. A slightly acid soil (pH6.5) is considered ideal, but only in unusual situations is plant growth adversely affected by extremes. In fact, although roses prefer a deeply prepared, good loam soil, they will do well in any soil that will produce good strong growth. They do not require heavy fertilization but thrive, as do all plants, on a balanced diet.

Before discussing the relative merits of "organic" and "inorganic" fertilizers, the two terms should probably be defined. The first refers to plant nutrients (humus or manures) derived from vegetation or animals, and the second, to the so-called chemical fertilizers that are derived mainly from other sources. A critical and unbiased analysis of the two will offer convincing proof that neither, in itself, is a cure-all for badly depleted soils and that both are usually required to promote maximum plant health, vigor and productiveness. The greatest value of organic manures is in improving the texture of the soil and in supplying many of the trace, or minor, elements required by plants. Their content of the major elements is so small that the amount required to induce maximum plant growth might prove toxic to some soils. In fact 20 pounds of ammonium sulphate will supply as much nitrogen to the soil as a ton of average manure.

The ash and nutrient contents of animal manures are controlled by several factors. Among these are the amount of hay, straw and other bedding or litter materials that they contain, the type and food of the animal or fowl that produced them, the age and the method of handling or composting. Well-rotted cow manure has long been recommended as the ideal food for roses, but its value is questionable, since several representative samples have shown an average analysis of only 0.32 per cent nitrogen, 0.15

per cent phosphorus, 0.47 per cent potash, and a few
minor elements. Fresh cow manure and that of fowls, hogs,
horses, rabbits and sheep are all superior in plant food
value. Dried, shredded and bagged manures now available
have a higher analysis than either fresh or rotted manures as
the loss of natural nutrients by leaching has been avoided,
and, in some instances, an increase has been effected by
the addition of inorganic fertilizers. However, they lack
the moisture-retentive qualities and, in many instances,
the humus-producing micro-organisms of barnyard manure.
This is probably the basis upon which we should evaluate
all barnyard manures, as inorganic fertilizers possess several times the nutrient value per pound, are easier to
apply, and, if both must be purchased, are less costly per
food unit. Although admittedly an excellent soil conditioner, the scarcity of barnyard manure in many areas is
also a deterring factor in its use. The elements it possesses
and which are not supplied by inorganic fertilizers can
be obtained, however, by working compost or humus-form-
ing materials such as partly decomposed straw, hay, sawdust, ground corn cobs, leaves, grass clippings or the more
permanent peat moss into the soil. Alfalfa, cotton seed,
soybean, bone or fish meal and tankage or degreased sludge
are accepted sources of slow-acting nutrients, but none
supply as many major and minor elements as economically
and in as readily available a form as the complete inorganic fertilizer.

There are certain major and minor, or trace, elements
that roses as well as other plants require, and each of
these serves a specific purpose in maintaining health, vigor

and productivity. The application of any, however, should not be excessive and *no fertilizer, either organic or inorganic, should be placed in direct contact with the roots or stems of the plant.* The major elements (nitrogen, phosphorus and potash) must be renewed frequently, but the trace elements are usually present, in sufficient quantities, in all soils having a reasonably high organic content.

If unhealthy or abnormal growth occurs and cannot be traced to a disease or other known cause, your County Agent or State Agricultural College should be consulted as they are familiar with the common soil deficiencies in your area. As residents of the state are not charged for advice, a detailed discussion of the symptoms of trace-element deficiency and the methods of correcting it is not presented here. If given, it might tend to confuse the inexperienced and a wrong analysis could be harmful.

Yearly mulches of fresh manure or other organic material will often correct the deficiency and this is probably the safest method to use for the purpose, as an overdose of chemical trace elements may prove fatal. Some of the more expensive inorganic mixtures now include the trace elements as well as the major ones, and, if used with discretion, are reasonably safe.

If the soil in which roses are planted contains a good supply of organic matter, no additional fertilization is required the first year. The advantages are apparent to anyone who has transplanted roses and has observed that a well-fed plant has a small root system in comparison to one that has been compelled to forage for food. Although most roses will bloom the first year, the flower production, during this period, should be considered secondary in importance to the development of a good root system. The latter will insure the future productivity and health of the plant.

The first feeding of established plants should be made when the leaf buds begin to swell in the spring; the second, at the close of the June blooming period; and the third, not later than two months before dormancy occurs in your area. Later feeding promotes late soft growth that is easily winter killed. A fistful of fertilizer evenly distributed around each plant should be sufficient, although the first application may be somewhat greater. For best and quickest results, the fertilizer should be worked into the soil and the bed well watered.

The supplying of plant nutrients through the foliage has proven quite effective and is accomplished by spraying specially prepared liquid fertilizer on the leaves. It should be done as recommended by the manufacturer. It is impossible to suggest one inorganic fertilizer formula that is best suited for roses as the requirements of one garden differ greatly from those of another. For naturally poor soil in northern Ohio, where roses have been grown continuously for more than twenty-five years, a 3 per cent nitrogen, 18 per cent phosphorus and 9 per cent potash mixture has proven very satisfactory. This is a standard farm-crop fertilizer that is always obtainable and inexpensive.

As a different formula may prove superior in another garden, it is probably advisable to outline briefly the function of each of the major elements, the symptoms of deficiency, and the means by which the deficiency may be corrected.

Nitrogen causes vegetative growth and should therefore be supplied most freely during early spring when the plant is building its framework. An oversupply during mid-summer and autumn may cause root injury and encourage the production of vigorous new growth that will not mature before the arrival of severe weather. A deficiency is apparent in small, soft, light-colored foliage, small flowers, weak, thin stems and general lack of vigor. The most popular nitrogenous fertilizers are: ammonium sulphate, ammonium nitrate, sodium nitrate, calcium nitrate, and ammonium phosphate. Ammonium nitrate should be applied at the rate of about ½ pound per 100 square feet, and the others at about double that amount. Ammonium phosphate is high in both nitrogen and phosphorus, and both elements are in a readily available form.

Phosphorus encourages root development, healthy foliage, good bloom production and aids in the full maturity of the plant. It is required throughout the season. When there is a deficiency, the growth is poor, blossom production scant, and the foliage may have a bronze or purplish hue. A pronounced lack will usually result in winter injury, as proper maturity of the stems is essential in the colder regions. Super phosphate and ammonium phosphate are the most rapidly acting sources, but should be worked deeply into the soil as they penetrate slowly. Tankage, fish, blood and cottonseed meal, ground tobacco stems, manure, raw and steamed bonemeal are among the organic sources.

Potash (Potassium), if lacking, results in generally

poor growth, slender weak stems, poor blossom color and
leaves that often have brown or yellow blotches along the
margins. When available in sufficient amounts, it promotes
the general health and vigor of the plant by building
strong plant calls and also aids in the assimilation of other
elements. Poorly drained, heavily cropped, extremely
sandy, highly alkaline and many of the reddish clay soils
of the South are often deficient. Plants require considerable quantities of potash, but an excess will cause premature hardening of growth and stunting. Potash at the rate
of 1 pound to 100 square feet, or wood ashes at the rate of
4 to 6 pounds is sufficient. Ground tobacco stems, cottonseed meal, manure and other organic materials also contain potash.

The above explanation of organic and inorganic fertilizers is given for the benefit of those readers who would
like to know a few of the "why's" of soil condition. However, to the many who have limited space and but a few
hours of leisure, be assured that good roses can be grown
with little more than peat moss to supply humus and a
complete chemical fertilizer such as 4-12-4 for the necessary plant food.

chapter three

Where and how
to plant

Roses will tolerate much abuse but cannot thrive in locations that are poorly drained, too shady, or where tree roots will encroach on their territory. All of these factors should be considered when selecting a site for a rose bed.

Ample drainage is probably the most important, as no rose can grow satisfactorily or survive for long in a soil that is continually wet. Such a soil becomes too compact and provides an unhealthy environment for the roots as they cannot develop or function properly. Harmful microorganisms which produce substances that are toxic to plants are also usually present in water-logged soils. Even though the plant should survive these hazards, it will probably succumb during the winter. If water does not remain on the soil surface after a rain, you can be reasonably sure that drainage is satisfactory. A practical method of

testing during dry weather is to dig a hole about 15 inches
deep and fill it with water. The rapidity of seepage is, of
course, dependent on the texture of the soil, but even in
heavy clay soils, the water should disappear in 4 or 5
hours. If this test proves that drainage is insufficient, you
have but two alternatives—either select another site or in-
stall drain tile.

While it is not likely that you will need drain tile, provided the premises have been occupied before and you
have good vegetation surrounding you, it may be necessary
in some cases. Have the work done professionally, for it
is too much for the amateur to tackle.

As all plant growth results from the food produced by
the action of sunlight on the leaves, it is apparent that a
plant as vigorous and productive as the rose should receive at least 6 to 8 hours of sunlight daily. Full sunlight
throughout the day is desirable, although some roses retain
their blossom color better if protected from the sun during
its period of greatest intensity. Shade in the morning is
conducive to the development of some leaf diseases as the
foliage will remain wet with dew for a longer period. If
full exposure to sunlight is impossible, it is therefore
probably best to plant roses where it is available during
the forenoon.

Roses should not be planted where their roots must com-
pete with those of trees or vigorous shrubs for food and
moisture. If this cannot be avoided, all invading roots
should be removed from the bed, the soil revitalized and a
barrier of sheet metal or other lasting material placed ver-
tically at the edge nearest the offender.

A usually overlooked and often destructive enemy of the rose are extremely high winds. They may cause damage throughout the year and some protection is advisable where they are prevalent.

The outmoded emphasis on the presumed necessity of preparing a rose bed deeply and intricately has probably discouraged many a potential rose grower. Greater stress should be placed on other phases of rose culture, but the subject of bed preparation should not be entirely ignored. The antiquated procedures that were once considered necessary can be simplified, since the possibly slight advantages do not compensate for the additional labor and cost involved. In fact, some of the long-recommended practices are actually detrimental and therefore less suitable than the modern easy-to-accomplish methods.

For years many authorities insisted that the proper procedure in planting roses was as follows: Remove three feet of soil, put one foot of cinders or stone in the bottom to provide drainage, mix the surface or topsoil with rotted manure or peat moss and place over the rubble; then fill the hole with left-over subsoil and cart away the remainder. Lest you become involved in this backbreaking labor, I strongly advise you not to use this system. You can grow beautiful roses with a minimum of effort.

If the soil in your garden is of naturally good quality and average depth, or has been improved as suggested in Chapter II, it is capable of producing good roses without further preparation. Roses, however, grow best in a deeply prepared soil, and if the grower is sufficiently ambitious, he may further improve their quality by preparing the bed

to a depth of 15 to 18 inches. This is accomplished by removing the topsoil and breaking up the subsoil to the required depth. Manure or other organic matter and a small
amount of superphosphate will lighten and enrich the subsoil. Inverted sod may also be placed in the lower depths.
After the topsoil has been replaced the beds should be
given an opportunity to settle before planting.

The time-worn saying that "it is better to place a ten
cent plant in a dollar hole than a dollar plant in a ten cent
hole" is still good advice, as a rose, properly planted, will
more than justify the additional time and effort required.
The results of improper planting are evident for a long
time and the plant may never recover entirely. If a few
basic rules that apply to most other plants as well as to
roses are followed, the planting may be easily and successfully accomplished. The several steps are listed in the order in which they are performed, and planting distances
are suggested in the chapter on classes and varieties.

No. 1   Unpack the roses in a place where they are not ex-
        posed to the drying influence of sun or wind. If
        canes are shriveled on arrival, it is advisable to soak
        the entire plant in water or bury it in moist soil until
        they become plump. This may require a day or
        more, but it is necessary to overcome the handicap
        imposed on the plant by improper packing or delays
        in transit.

No. 2   Prune the tops (and remove all thin stems) to about
        12 inches above the crown and cut back all broken
        and damaged stems and roots to uninjured wood.
        (Most reliable nurseries ship their stock properly
        pruned and ready to plant, but a stem or root is
        sometimes broken in transit.) Don't prune the roots

to fit the hole but dig the hole to fit the roots, as rose root development is comparatively slow. A badly mutilated system may never completely recover. The understock stub that protrudes above the point where the desired variety was budded onto the understock should be trimmed back flush with the main stem. It is dead tissue and of no value. When removed, living tissue will strongly unite the rootstock and named variety, and the possibility of breakage or disease entrance at this point will be reduced. The beginner may hesitate to cut back the top to 12 inches, but during the first year, the roots are not capable of supporting long stems and also producing new ones from the crown. The latter are more important. After the foregoing operations are performed, the roses should be placed in a pail of water until they are planted.

No. 3   Dig the hole sufficiently large to accommodate the roots without crowding or coiling and place a small cone-shaped mound of earth in the center of it. Place the root system, spread out, on top of the mound which should be high enough to extend to the top or beginning of the system. Rose roots grow naturally downward and outward, and by placing them over a mound, the possibility of air pockets will be greatly avoided (Fig. 3a). This method eliminates the necessity of working the soil between the roots with the fingers. The depth of planting is a rather controversial subject but should be determined by the severity of the climate and the amount of winter protection the grower intends to apply. In regions where winter protection is required, the point where the stub was removed (the bud-union) should be about 1 inch below the surface. In others it may be level with or slightly above the bed level.

When planting potted roses, the outer roots should be uncoiled carefully so as to prevent injury to the small feeder roots and rapidly so that they will not be unduly exposed to drying. Plant immediately, give plenty of water, and protect from the sun and wind for a few days.

Roses may be moved, if absolutely necessary, during the growing season, provided the operations are performed hurriedly. Disturb the roots as little as possible by balling and burlaping, prune stems to compensate for loss of roots in digging, wrap the tops in wet burlap, and replant with all haste.

During the dormant season, do not hesitate to move a rose that appears to be unhappy in its present location. A new one may revitalize it.

No. 4   Fill the hole to an inch or two above the topmost roots with loose (not lumpy) soil and pour in water (Figs. 3b and c). The water will serve to eliminate air pockets and is much superior to tamping as this often causes the soil to become too compact and may damage the roots as well as set the plant too deeply. After the water has seeped through the soil, the hole may be filled.

No. 5   The next step is to mound soil to the top of the stems (Fig. 3d). In fall planting, this mound provides winter protection, and in spring planting, it serves to retain moisture in the stems until the roots have become established. When applied in the spring, it should be removed after about 2 weeks and preferably on a cloudy day. Burlap, spagnum moss or any other material that will shade the stems may be used in place of the mound, but for winter protection, there is no substitute for soil.

No. 6   Roses should be permanently tagged, or their location recorded, as soon as they are planted. Names are soon forgotten and as the interest in roses grows, the name of a variety becomes increasingly important. Even the expert may find it difficult to definitely identify a variety.

No. 7 Do not apply chemical fertilizers the first year as the roots are not sufficiently well established to absorb them. The slower-acting organic fertilizers may be used sparingly, but if the bed has been well prepared, they are unnecessary.

No. 8 Many benefits are derived by applying a 1½- to 2-inch mulch to the surface of the rose bed. It reduces labor by checking weed growth, prevents the puddling effect of rain, retains moisture, encourages the development of beneficial soil organisms, conditions the soil by building up the organic content, reduces the possibility of black-spot infection, and keeps the soil several degrees cooler.

Roses dislike hot weather and perform best during the cooler periods of the year. Bloom production during the hot summer months will be increased considerably by reducing the temperature of the soil.

Various materials may be used for mulching, and the determining factor should probably be their cost and availability in your locality. Those that pack so tightly as to form a water shedding surface are unsuitable and some absorb considerable nitrogen as they decompose. The nitrogen is later released but during the early periods of decomposing, it may be advantageous to add extra nitrogen to a bed mulched with them. Moisture-retaining mulches should not be placed next to stems as they may induce disease development.

A brief summary of the most generally used materials follows:

BUCKWHEAT HULLS Stay in place, do not pack, permit free penetration of water and are attractive. Somewhat costly in some regions.

COTTONSEED HULLS Suitable and attractive.

GROUND CORN COBS A fine soil conditioner, easily

applied and attractive. Extra nitrogen may be
needed.

LAWN CLIPPINGS   Suitable but deteriorate rapidly.

LEAVES   Usually disappear before the end of summer unless application is heavy.

MANURE   Possesses considerable value, but is both
odorous and unsightly.

PEANUT SHELLS   Suitable.

PEAT MOSS   Attractive and easily applied, but costly
and has a tendency to absorb moisture before it
reaches the soil.

PINE NEEDLES   Very good where available.

SAWDUST   Should be at least 3 years old or it will
absorb considerable nitrogen. Attractive, cheap
and a good soil conditioner.

STRAW   Difficult to place, requires added nitrogen
and should be applied heavily as it settles considerably.

Roses planted in a mulched bed require little summer
care other than the removal of faded flowers, an occasional
dusting or spraying to prevent injury by disease or pests,
and watering. They do not demand an excessive amount
of water but will benefit by an occasional ground soaking.
Faded flowers are unsightly and the food required to produce seeds may better be diverted to other plant func-
tions. Cut back to the first complete, or five-foliated, leaf
(Fig. 9).

METHODS   Growing roses is not difficult provided the
proper tools are available for a given job (Fig. 1). The
hole to receive the plant can be dug with a spade or spading fork, and a shovel is used to place the remaining soil
around the plant. Most gardeners prefer long handles,
which are less of a strain on back muscles.

A wheelbarrow is of great value, and is always handy for hauling tools, garden hose, plants, fertilizer and the like. With the addition of a garden hoe you can use it to mix conditioners thoroughly with topsoil.

Always use the best available pruning shears for roses. They must be made of good steel to hold a sharp cutting

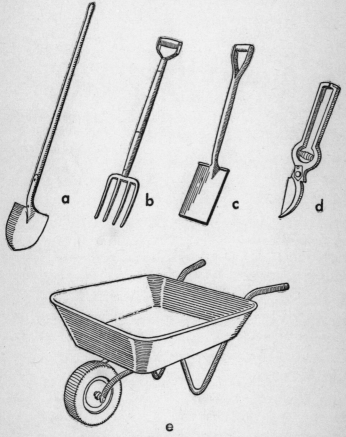

1. Tools. *a) Shovel. b) Spading Fork. c) Spade. d) Pruning Shears. e) Wheelbarrow.*

edge. Shears that crush instead of cutting lead to trouble.

SETTING THE PLANTS No matter how careful your preparations have been, they will come to nothing if your roses are planted too shallow or too deep (Fig. 2). Setting them at the proper height will contribute to greater success.

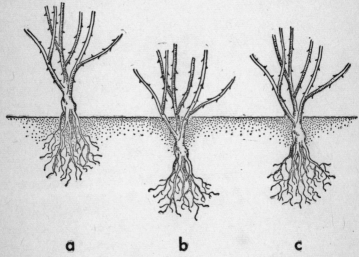

a   b   c

2. Planting. *a) Too high. b) Too low. c) Correct depth in severe climates but may be higher where winter protection is not necessary.*

FIRMING THE SOIL For years gardeners have used foot pressure to firm soil around their plants. Now, however, many authorities prefer the watering-in method to remove air pockets (Fig. 3).

WATERING Never water roses from above with a sprinkler or a hose with a nozzle. The pressure damages blossoms and washes away protective dusts and sprays. Wet foliage is an invitation to disease. During extremely dry

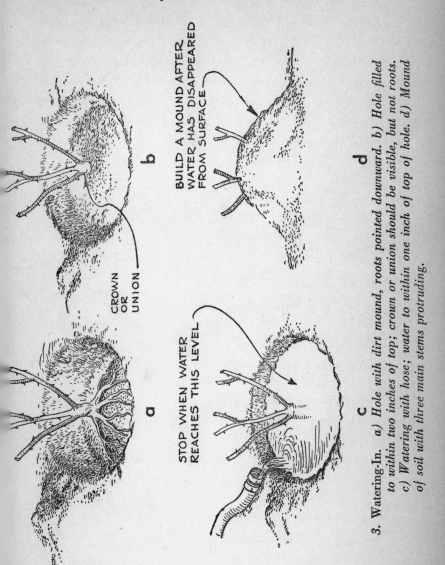

CROWN OR UNION

STOP WHEN WATER REACHES THIS LEVEL

BUILD A MOUND AFTER WATER HAS DISAPPEARED FROM SURFACE

a

b

c

d

3. Watering-In. *a) Hole with dirt mound, roots pointed downward. b) Hole filled to within two inches of top; crown or union should be visible, but not roots. c) Watering with hose; water to within one inch of top of hole. d) Mound of soil with three main stems protruding.*

weather when watering is necessary, place the end of your
hose, without the nozzle, in the middle of a good-sized
board laid level so that the water flows gently over all
sides (Fig. 4). Use low water pressure, and be sure the soil
gets a good soaking. Shallow watering is worse than none
at all; it causes the feeder roots to turn up into hot soil,
rather than remain deep where it is cooler.

4. Watering.

Roses will thrive without coddling, but intelligent care
will be repaid in greater plant vigor and bloom production.

chapter four

Buying roses

The purchase of well-grown and properly handled stock from a reputable dealer is one of the most important factors in successful rose culture. Exceptionally low-priced roses are rarely a good investment and usually result in needless losses and discouragement. The temptation to buy them is often difficult to resist and, although they may survive if given adequate care, they represent a gamble that only an experienced and persevering gardener should attempt. However, in their defense, it must be admitted that many now successful and enthusiastic rose growers obtained their first experience by planting them.

Bargain roses usually consist of undersized, poorly rooted, misnamed, improperly handled, too old or damaged roses that a reputable dealer would not sell under his name. Spent greenhouse roses that are often not adapted to outdoor culture are occasionally bundled and offered at remarkably low prices.

These collections should not be confused with those listed in the catalogs of several rose nurserymen. The latter represent very good value, especially for the beginner, as they include reliable and popular varieties that justify propagation in large quantities. They are not culls, and the primary objective in selling them is to offer a low-priced collection of attractive sure-to-succeed varieties. This is often an inducement to the beginner who does not care to make a large investment in his initial venture, and it frequently results in future sales for the one selling them.

The location of the nursery from which you purchase your roses is relatively unimportant as reliable growers are not confined to any one geographical area. It is sometimes presumed that a rose from California or Texas is not adapted to culture in the North, but this is not true. In fact, several Eastern and Central states nurseries maintain growing fields or sell roses that were propagated in more moderate climates. In a few instances, the rootstock of roses obtained from small Southern or Pacific Coast growers that cater to local trade may not be sufficiently hardy in your state. This should be ascertained before your order is placed and, if the variety and rootstock are adaptable, the source is less important than the quality of the stock.

The surest way to success is to buy only two-year-old, field-grown, dormant No.-1-grade stock from a nurseryman who has the facilities and knowledge to properly dig and handle it. The method of grading is somewhat elastic, but a rose classified as No. 1 should have 3 or more sturdy stems (No. 1½ has 2, and No. 2, 1 stem), and a good root system. The latter is more important than the number and size of stems, and a plant graded as No. 1, in respect to the stems, may have a badly mutilated root system and not be as good an investment as a carefully dug 1½ grade plant. A No.-2-grade plant has not developed properly in the nursery and, due to some defect, probably never will.

Many of the roses sold in stores that do not specialize in nursery stock have not been properly handled. The roots have probably dried and the stems are either dry or have produced shoots that have used up considerable plant energy. Invariably the beginner will overlook this fact and select the plant with the most and longest shoots as he assumes this is evidence of inherent vigor. A plant that has retained its dormancy, however, is much more likely to survive. Even though the stems are slightly withered, plumpness may often be restored by completely covering the plant with damp soil for a few days.

You can be sure that you are buying good stock if you patronize a reputable dealer, or, if in doubt, by consulting another rose grower. He will gladly discuss roses, where and what to purchase, and may supply helpful tips on their culture.

There is considerable disagreement as to whether roses should be planted in the spring or the fall. This is influenced to a great extent by personal opinion and the part of the country in which they are to be grown. In either event, it is advisable to place the order in the fall as preferred varieties are often unavailable in the spring. Shipment may not be possible, or desired, until spring, but you will be certain of receiving better plants of the varieties you desire and at the proper time for planting in your region.

If you are opposed to fall planting, the roses may be received at that time, placed in a trench (in a well-drained location) and covered with soil until spring. They will be on hand when you want them and will be in better condition than those that have spent the winter under nursery storage conditions.

Roses are sometimes received when weather conditions, or other causes, prevent their immediate planting. When this occurs, the unopened package can be stored in a cool place for a few days. If there is a longer delay, it is advisable to remove them from the package and cover with soil until they can be planted.

Fall vs. spring planting—a few comments follow, but near-by rose growers should be consulted as to the most suitable time in your region.

FOR FALL PLANTING   There is usually less other garden work, the weather is more pleasant, and the soil is in better condition. Roots have been out of the ground a shorter period of time and become partially established before the ground freezes. The June bloom is usually earlier and better. A larger selection of varieties is available, and if a poor bush is received, there is time to exchange it for another. Planting may proceed from the time plants are received until the ground freezes.

FOR SPRING PLANTING   It is not necessary to protect the roses for the winter and losses from intermittent thawing and freezing are avoided. Fall planted roses may not be sufficiently hardened to withstand the cold. Below freezing temperatures will not arrive unexpectedly and cause injury. Warm days in late fall may encourage growth that will later freeze. Some varieties are not available until spring. Planting can begin as soon as the ground is workable. Late spring planting is not advisable, however, as the roots should be established before the arrival of hot weather. When this is necessary, potted roses should be purchased as they are superior to bare rootstock that has been held too long in storage.

826859

chapter five

Classes and varieties

The selection of proper varieties is vitally important as there are roses, in all classes, that are not as reliable, thrifty or disease resistant as others. The beginner should not be unduly influenced by the frequently exaggerated descriptions of the new introductions. They may justify the praise they are given, but there are many older, less costly varieties that are equally attractive and have proven their worth for many years.

The fact that a rose is patented is no guarantee that it is superior to one that is not. However, when the letters AARS follow the name, they signify that the variety has been tested for at least two years in different parts of the country and has proven to be exceptionally good. Only the best roses receive this award.

The American Rose Society performs a valuable service

to all rose growers by publishing an annual buying guide in which varieties of the hybrid tea, floribunda and climber classes are given national ratings. A rating of 10 is considered perfect, 9 to 10 outstanding, 8 to 8.9 excellent, and 7 to 7.9 good. Varieties receiving lower ratings have one or more pronounced deficiencies and should be avoided by the beginner. As these ratings are based on reports received from correspondents in various parts of the United States and Canada, they are of unquestionable value. Complete copies of this list may be obtained by sending a stamped, self-addressed envelope to the American Rose Society, 4048 Roselea Place, Columbus, 14, Ohio. In fact, why not become a member? The dues are moderate, the benefits many, and 99 per cent of the 15,000 membership are amateur growers like yourself.

The following list comprises the better varieties in each class with a brief description of the class and the purposes for which it is best adapted. Detailed descriptions of the popular varieties are unnecessary as they appear in most rose catalogs, and the prospective purchaser invariably obtains one or more of these before placing his order. The figures following the class titles are suggested planting distances. In warm climates where bushes grow quite large and in regions where winter protection is required, the maximum distance should be used when planting the tender varieties in beds. Closely planted roses may create a more pleasing effect but require more fertilization, are more subject to disease, and earth must be hauled in for winter protective mounds. Roses that have proven to be hardy without protection in northern Ohio, where temperatures occasionally fall below zero and snow cover is usually light, are so designated. Specified heights are relative to the class and refer to roses grown under average conditions. The blossom color of a rose may vary somewhat under different conditions and general, rather than specific, colors are stated in the following lists. In other words, a rose classed as red may be red, crimson, carmine, scarlet, cinnabar or hues of any of these colors.

Hybrid teas (18"-24")

Approximately 75 per cent of the roses now grown are members of this class, which includes varieties of various colors and forms. Their popularity is justified as they are undoubtedly the most attractive of all roses, bloom repeatedly and, with adequate winter protection, can be grown throughout the United States. The average ultimate growth is from 2 to 3 feet, but under ideal conditions, some varieties may attain 5 or 6 feet.

New varieties are being introduced at such a rapid rate that it is difficult to suggest a beginner's list of any permanent value. The following is too brief to include all the good ones, but does record those of definite value.

> RED
> *Charlotte Armstrong (9.0)*
> *Christopher Stone (8.8)*
> *Crimson Glory (9.5)*
> *Etoile de Hollande (8.9)*
> *Grand Duchesse Charlotte (8.3)*
> *Red Duchess (7.9)*
> *Red Radiance (8.0)*

McGredy's Scarlet (7.9)
Tallyho (8.3)
Texas Centennial (7.9)

PINK
Betty Uprichard (7.9)
Comtesse Vandal (8.0)
Curly Pink (8.2)
Good News (8.0)
Mrs. Charles Bell (8.0)
Picture (8.4)
Pink Princess (8.1)
Radiance (8.2)
Show Girl (8.2)
The Doctor (7.9)

YELLOW
Buccaneer (8.4)
Debonair (7.9)
Eclipse (8.5)
Golden Dawn (8.1)
Soeur Therese (7.9)

WHITE
Kaiserin Auguste Viktoria (7.2)
McGredy's Ivory (7.8)
Mme. Jules Bouche (7.3)
Pedralbes (8.0)
Rex Anderson (7.1)

BLENDS
Condesa de Sastago (7.9). Red and yellow
Duquesa de Penaranda (7.9). Orange Blends
Good News (8.4). Pink, apricot
Mme. Henri Guillot (8.9). Orange, coral, red
Peace (9.4). Yellow, pink edged

Polyanthas and floribundas (12"-36")

These closely related cluster-flowering classes are com-
bined in most catalogs as they are adapted to the same
general purpose; that is, for accent points in the shrub
border or foundation planting, for individual or mass
planting, hedges, and for any other purpose where an extremely floriferous plant is desired.

The varieties differ considerably in stature and hardiness and this should be ascertained before the order is
placed. Generally the small-flowered sorts are the most
hardy, but there is no relationship between blossom size and
vigor. Both large- and small-flowering varieties, from single to very double, are available in a wide range of colors
and heights from 10 inches to 6 or 7 feet. As a whole,
they are more hardy, floriferous and disease resistant
than the hybrid teas. The asterisk (*) indicates that the
variety is comparatively hardy. Heights are average. Rating is given if available.

Betty Prior (8.8). Carmine-pink, single, 3 feet
Cameo. Salmon, semi-double, 1½ feet
 Carrousel (9.1). Dark red, semi-double, 2½ feet
Dagmar Spath (8.2). White, semi-double, 1½ feet
Donald Prior (8.6). Scarlet, semi-double, 3½ feet
Else Poulsen (8.7). Rose pink, single, 2½ feet
 Fashion (9.5). Coral peach, double, 2 feet
 Floradora (8.2). Cinnabar red, double, 3½ feet
Frensham (8.2). Red, semi-double, 2½ feet spreading
Gloria Mundi. Orange-scarlet, double, 3 feet
 Goldilocks (7.9). Yellow, double, 2 feet
 Ma Perkins (7.2). Coral red, double, 3 feet
Margo Koster (8.8). Orange-red, double, 1 foot

*_Ming Toy_ (7.7). Rose pink, double, 3 feet
 Pinnochio (7.6). Salmon pink, double, 2½ feet
 Red Pinnochio (8.7). Carmine red, double, 2½ feet
*_Red Ripples_ (7.8). Red, semi-double, 2½ feet
 Rosenelfe (8.9). Pink, double, 2 feet
*_Summer Snow_ (8.4). White, semi-double, 2½ feet
*_The Fairy_ (9.3). Pink, double, compact, spreading 1½ feet

Hybrid perpetuals (24"-36")

The hybrid perpetual roses constitute a link between the roses of the early part of the nineteenth century and those of today. As a group they are somewhat hardier and more sturdy than the hybrid teas, but the blossom production is negligible after June. They will thrive where others, more exacting, will fail, but they do require winter protection in the Northern states.

The so-called "pegging down" method of growing roses is particularly well adapted to members of this class. Remove all but 3 or 4 of the most vigorous stems, bend these slowly to a horizontal position and tie to stakes so that they are about one foot above the ground. This results in the production of lateral shoots along the stems rather than at the top only, and the yield of flowers is increased considerably. Stems should be renewed annually or at least every two years. If retained, the laterals should be cut back to within one or two eyes of the main stem.

The blossoms of the hybrid perpetuals are usually large and globular in form. The color range is from white to deep maroon, but does not include the yellow shades.

No white rose of any class is as desirable as vigorous

Frau Karl Druschki, and, fortunately, this variety blooms quite consistently throughout the summer. Others of importance are:

> *General Jaqueminot.* Red, 4 to 5 feet
> *George Arends.* Pink, 3 feet
> *Mrs. John Laing.* Pink, 3 feet
> *Paul Neyron.* Pink, extremely large, 4 feet
> *Prince Camille de Rohan.* Crimson maroon, 2½ feet
> *Roger Lambelin.* Bright crimson margined or streaked white, 2½ feet
> *Ulrich Brunner.* Geranium red, 3½ feet
> *Victor Verdier.* Bright carmine, 2½ feet

Tea roses .(North 1½'-2'; South 3'-5')

These roses are of greatest value in Southern gardens as they require a shorter rest period than most roses. The wood ripens so slowly that it frequently winter kills unless well protected in regions where the temperature falls below 25 degrees. They are more disease resistant than the hybrid teas, but the blossom stems of many varieties are weak and, during extremely hot weather, the blossoms have a tendency to ball and rot. Production is exceptionally abundant throughout the summer. The semi-double to double, intensely fragrant flowers are mostly blends and shades of soft pink and light yellow. Where no winter injury occurs, it is not unusual to see plants that are 6 feet tall, but in the North, they rarely exceed 2 feet. Pruning should be confined to the removal of dead and weak growth. Ultimate heights are not specified as they are influenced by the climate.

Baroness Henriette Snoy. Peach-pink shaded cream
Duchesse de Brabant. Shell pink
Maman Cochet. Clear pink
Marie van Houtte. Canary yellow, pink tipped
Mme. Lombard. Dark pink-shaded salmon
Mme. Melanie Soupert. Salmon yellow
Mrs. Dudley Cross. Light yellow
Safrano. Saffron yellow.

China roses (18"-36")

A greatly neglected class that possesses several desirable attributes. The blossoms are small in comparison to those of the hybrid teas, but the plants are more hardy, extremely floriferous and practically disease resistant. They compare favorably with the average polyantha or floribunda in blossom size and the plants may be used for the same purpose. Prune lightly and protect only where temperatures lower than 5 degrees above zero occur frequently.

Cramoisi Supérieur. Crimson, double, 3 feet
Ducher. White, double, 2 feet
Fabvier. Crimson, semi-double, 2½ feet
Hermosa. Light blush pink, double, 2 feet
Hofgartner Kalb. Carmine, double, 3 feet
R. Chinensis (Old Blush). Blush pink, double, height variable
R. Chinensis Mutabilis. The single flowers open yellow, change to orange, then red and finally crimson, 3 feet
R. Chinensis Serratipetala. Red, fringed petals, double, 3 feet
R. Chinensis Viridiflora (Green Rose). Double, an interesting oddity, 2 feet

Miniature roses (6"-10")

These small replicas of the larger everblooming roses are becoming increasingly popular as they may be used for many purposes. They are at home in the rock garden, are suitable for edging and will thrive in a flowerpot or window box. A thimble will accommodate five or more and they are ideal as corsage material, for hair adornment, or as a boutonnière. The majority are quite hardy, but the plants should be mulched to prevent heaving during periods of alternate thawing and freezing. The dwarf characteristic is best retained if they are not fed excessively. The following produce double flowers:

Baby Gold Star. Small, golden yellow, 10 to 12 inches
Bo-Peep. Rose red, 6 to 8 inches
Cinderella. White, 6 to 8 inches
Midget. Deep rose, 4 to 5 inches
Pixie. White, 6 to 8 inches
Red Elf. Dark red, 4 to 5 inches
Red Imp. Crimson, 5 to 6 inches
R. Rouletii. Bright pink, 6 to 8 inches
Sweet Fairy. Deep pink, 8 to 10 inches
Tom Thumb. Crimson, 4 to 6 inches

Old-fashioned roses

A group of hardy and sturdy roses that possess considerable attractiveness and sentimental value; however, they are rarely recurrent—that is, they usually bloom only once a season. In addition to those discussed under the China, tea and shrub rose groups, the following double-flowering varieties are desirable:

Cabbage Rose (R. centifolia). Light pink
Camaieux. Blush pink, splashed vivid crimson
Cardinal de Richelieu. Grayish mauve
Gloire des Mousseux. Carmine, mossy
Hebes Lip. White, edged rosy crimson, semi-double
Jeanne de Montfort. Pink, edged silver
Konigin von Danemark. Flesh pink, dark pink center
Mme. Hardy. White
Tricolore de Flandre. Lilac white with red stripes
Tuscany. Dark crimson purple, semi-double

Species roses

When the letter R precedes the name of a rose, it desig-
nates that it is a species, or wild rose, rather than a horticultural variety. The blossoms, usually single, are produced freely in early summer and denote a simplicity and
beauty that is lacking in the blossoms of our modern roses.
The plants are graceful and charming and their beauty is
further enhanced by the attractive seed pods that ornament
the plant during summer and fall.

In addition to those listed under shrub roses, the following are desirable:

R. Alba. Semi-double white, intensely fragrant, 6 feet
R. Moyesii. Single, blood red, temperamental but beautiful,
10 feet
R. Omiensis. Single, 4-petaled, white, attractive thorns, 10
feet
R. Palustris. Single pink, will grow in swampy spots, 8 feet
R. Primula. Single yellow, 6 to 8 feet

Shrub roses

The value of the shrub type roses has never been fully
appreciated. Surely they have more to offer than many of
the shrubs used as landscape material and are available in
a wider variety of blossom color. The majority are sturdy,
hardy plants that bloom heavily once a year, require but
little attention, and are not too particular as to soil or location. No other shrub can offer more. Shrub roses are
adapted to many uses formerly thought unsuitable for
roses. Among these are impregnable hedges, living fences,
to screen unsightly areas, in the border, or, as specimens.

Birds prefer them to other shrubs for nesting and enjoy
eating the seeds as much as you will enjoy watching the
seed pods develop and assume rich coloring in late summer and fall. The following list contains but a few of the
many roses suitable for landscape use:

Autumn Bouquet. Pink, double, repeats, 4 to 5 feet, moderately hardy

Blanc Double de Coubert. White, double, repeats, 5 feet,
hardy

Crested Moss. Pink, double, interesting blooms, 5 feet, hardy

Fragrant Beauty. Carmine red, similar to Autumn Bouquet

F. J. Grootendorst. Red, carnationlike flowers, repeats, 5 feet,
hardy

Harison's Yellow. Deep yellow, double, an old favorite, 6
feet, hardy

Hon. Lady Lindsay. Buff yellow, double, repeats, 3 feet, moderately hardy

Kazanlik. Pink, semi-double, very fragrant, 4 feet, hardy

Mabelle Stearns. Peach pink, double, repeats, height about 2
feet but spreads to 6 feet or more, hardy

Maiden's Blush. Soft blush, semi-double, 7 feet, hardy

Nevada. White, single, 7 feet, requires protection in the North

Old Blush. See China Roses

Pink Grootendorst. Pink form of F. J. Grootendorst

Rosa Mundi. Variegated white, pink and red, semi-double, 3 feet, hardy

R. Hugonis. Yellow, single, very early, prefers poor soil, 5 to 10 feet, hardy

R. Roxburghii. Pale pink, single or double, interesting and attractive fruits, bark and foliage. The single form is hardy and reaches 6 to 8 feet. The double form is less vigorous and hardy

R. Rubrifolia. Small, single pink blossoms, attractive purplish foliage, 6 feet, hardy

R. Spinosissima. White, single, freely produced, 3 feet, hardy

R. Spinosissima Altaica. White, single, 6 feet, very hardy

Salet. Rose pink, double, mossy buds, repeats, 5 feet, hardy

Sanguinaire. Dark red, semi-double, repeats, 6 feet, requires protection

Stanwell Perpetual. Pink, double, repeats, 3 to 4 feet, hardy

Creeping roses (5'-7')

A type of rose that grows best when planted where it may trail over banks, boulders or low walls. May also be grown on posts if wrapped around spirally, but most varieties are less hardy when not in close contact with the soil. If planted on a steep bank, a shelf-like depression should be made and surrounded with stones. This will retain soil and moisture around the roots.

Carpet of Gold. Double, yellow

Coral Creeper. Apricot to pink, semi-double

Little Compton Creeper. Single, deep pink

R. Wichuraiana. Single, white, very vigorous

Max Graf. Large, single, pink

Tree roses

Tree, or standard, roses are produced by budding, or grafting another variety on the stem of a vigorous growing rose. They are attractive and effective as accent points, but are costly and liable to injury by high winds if not securely tied to a stake. Not recommended for culture in the North as they must either be buried or otherwise well protected during the winter. Pruning should consist of cutting back all stems to 6 to 12 inches from their base and removing completely all stems that grow from the roots or trunk below the point where the plants were joined.

Climbing roses

These rampant-growing members of the rose family have much to recommend their greater usage. The more vigorous varieties may be used to transform an ugly wall into an asset, enhance the value of a plain fence, partially conceal an unattractive view, provide shade when trained on an arbor, serve as a hedge, and, if planted closely together, they form a windbreak or snow fence. The pillar types, when trained on a post, break the monotony of a formal garden by giving height and are more satisfactory and less expensive than tree roses. The purposes to which the group is adapted are somewhat similar, but the members differ greatly in flowering characteristics and should be pruned differently. For this reason, they are separated into three groups: climbers, ramblers and pillars.

Climbers are varieties of rather stiff growth that produce blossom-bearing shoots at or near the top of the previous year's growth. The following are desirable varieties:

Blaze. Scarlet, semi-double, repeats
City of York. White, semi-double
Doubloons. Yellow, double, may repeat, not dependably hardy
Dream Girl. Pink, double, repeats, requires protection
Dr. Huey. Maroon, semi-double, may require protection
Dr. W. van Fleet. Pink, double, very vigorous
Golden Glow. Yellow, double
New Dawn. Pink, double, repeats
Paul's Scarlet. Scarlet, semi-double
Silver Moon. White, semi-double, vigorous, not dependably hardy

A rambler has long, thin, pliable canes which, if not supported, are of more or less procumbent habit of growth. Many of the varieties are extremely susceptible to mildew and, for this reason, the group is rapidly losing favor. *Bloomfield Courage* (single, velvety red with white center) and *Chevy Chase* (double, dark crimson) are recommended.

The pillar roses are less vigorous than either of the preceding. The climbing hybrid teas, polyanthas and floribundas are included in this group as well as many of the less vigorous climbers, such as *Blaze, Dream Girl, Mary Wallace, Doubloons, Glenn Dale* and *Mrs. Whitman Cross.*
Climbing descendants of bush roses produce similar blossoms, but less freely, and are not dependably hardy in

the North. If frozen back, they usually fail to bloom the following year. *Crimson Glory, Christopher Stone, Golden Dawn, Summer Snow* and *Gloria Mundi* have produced interesting climbing counterparts.

chapter six

Diseases and pests

The contents of this chapter may possibly deter the timid or pessimistic flower lover from planting roses, but no book devoted to the culture of the rose would serve its purpose if a chapter on diseases and pests were not included. It is hoped that the preceding chapters have aroused the necessary enthusiasm and that this discussion will serve its intended purpose—to describe briefly the various major enemies of the rose and suggest practical and easy methods of controlling them. Other horticultural subjects also have specific enemies and if the reader has succeeded in combating them, he should be equally successful with those that attack the rose. In fact, he will probably be better able to do so as the long-continued popularity and commercial value of the rose has encouraged an intensive and specialized study of the diseases and pests that afflict it. The information gained has resulted in the development of numerous simplified and effective methods of control.

No rose garden will ever be host to all the recorded enemies; few are serious, and all can be prevented from attaining epidemic proportions by using certain precautionary measures and by establishing a regular spraying or dusting program. It is much easier to prevent an infestation than to eradicate it, and effective control methods are no more difficult than ineffective ones.

The preservation throughout the growing season of a maximum amount of healthy uninjured foliage is the major objective in disease and pest control. Premature defoliation causes poor growth during the season when the plants would otherwise be vigorous. In the late summer, such plants may be stimulated to increased vegetative growth and, as this requires large quantities of food, the stored reserves are seriously depleted. Although the plant may survive the winter, the effects are usually apparent during the early part of the following season. This late growth is of little value as it rarely has an opportunity to mature before the advent of severe temperatures.

Garden sanitation and the maintenance of soil fertility sufficient to induce maximum plant health are important factors in preventing or reducing injury by insects and disease. All diseased portions of the plant should be burned, and weeds, which often serve as host plants, should be eliminated. Some diseases may be introduced into a garden on new plants, all of which should be examined carefully before planting. Those obviously diseased should be rejected and doubtful ones examined by a more experienced grower or the experts of your State Agricultural College. Abnormal growths on the crowns or roots of roses and other plants may seriously infest your soil.

Spraying or dusting may be compared to an insurance policy and should be regular and thorough whether infestation is apparent or not. The regularity of application is dependent, to some extent, on weather conditions, the disease or pest you are combating, and the degree of infestation. The beginner may well establish a policy of dusting or spraying once a week (from the time the first leaves unfurl until late summer) with one of the several multipurpose materials now available. They do not destroy every insect and disease that might appear, but they do prevent them from becoming disastrous, and so simplify the problem of control. These materials may appear to be somewhat costly as they contain ingredients that are probably not needed in your particular garden. However, they do offer release from worry and are sold by most nurserymen, seedsmen, and farm-supply houses. If the cost is seemingly prohibitive and you prefer to mix your own, the following combinations have proven effective.

A reliable, economical and easy-to-prepare dust for the control of most leaf-chewing insects and diseases is composed of 9 parts dusting sulfur (325 mesh or finer) and 1 part powdered lead arsenate. One part fresh nicotine dust (3 or 4 per cent) may be added for aphid control. Mix thoroughly and do not apply when temperature exceeds 85 degrees as leaf burn may result. The primary purpose of all fungicides and insecticides is to preserve rather than destroy the foliage. Incidentally, disease-producing organisms are less active during prolonged periods of hot, dry weather. If you prefer a spray, dissolve 1 teaspoonful of a detergent in 3 gallons of water and add 3 tablespoons of fermate and $1\frac{1}{2}$ tablespoons each of 50 per cent wettable DDT and wettable sulfur. Mix thoroughly.

The simplicity of disease control is evidenced by the fact that only five diseases—black spot, powdery mildew, rust, canker and crown gall—are ordinarily of major importance. The first three are controlled by the same fungicide and this is also indirectly effective for the fourth. The last is less likely to be a problem.

Insect pests are separated into two categories: those that chew the blossoms or foliage, and those that suck the plant juices. The former are destroyed by stomach poisons, and the latter by materials that adhere to their bodies. The multi-purpose sprays and dusts contain ingredients for the control of most insects as well as diseases.

We often overlook the fact that birds are valuable allies in reducing the insect population. Birdhouses designed to attract insect-eating birds and a strategically located bird-bath, or drinking fountain, will induce them to frequent your garden.

The amateur gardener is often in doubt as to whether a spray or dust is best. This is understandable as there are advantages to each. In either event, certain fundamentals of effective and safe disease and pest control should be known and heeded. They are:

(1) The material should be applied with equipment

capable of distributing it on both surfaces of the leaves, as several insects feed mainly on the underside and many disease organisms enter there.

(2) New growth should be protected as it develops, insects should be destroyed before they become numerous, and a fungicide should be on the foliage before infection occurs.

(3) Applications are made preferably on the first clear day following a heavy rain when the foliage is dry and the winds are not too strong.

(4) Applications should be light so that only the merest trace can be seen on the foliage.

(5) In combining or mixing materials, follow directions carefully.

(6) Several insecticides and some fungicides are toxic to humans and pets; use them with caution and as directed by the manufacturer.

The spray-vs.-dust discussion is of long standing, but the pros and cons may be summarized in a few words. Dusting is more easily accomplished as no mixing is required and there is no equipment to clean. It therefore tends to prevent procrastination. Dusting is possibly slightly less effective, but two dusts can be applied while one spray is being prepared. Contrary to general opinion, a dust will cover adequately and more evenly when the foliage is dry and it will survive several light rains. In the control of some pests and diseases, a spray is preferable as a few very desirable materials are not, at the present, available in dust form. Equipment does not differ greatly in cost and either method is capable of successfully controlling the following major and most important minor diseases and pests. Some typical sprayers and dusters are shown in Figs. 5 and 6.

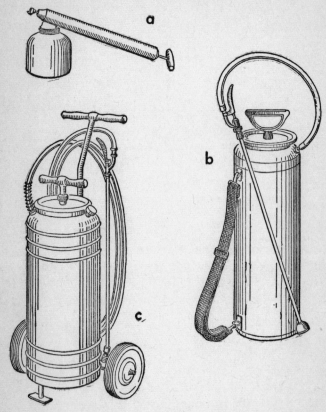

5. Sprayers. *a) One-quart Copper. b) Four-gallon Galvanized Steel. c) Five-gallon Cart Sprayer. The four-gallon size is carried on the shoulder by means of the strap. Pressure is created in b) and c) by pumping with the top handle, after which they continue to operate for some time, the flow being controlled by a trigger; c) may also be used for washing cars, windows, etc., as well as for insecticides and weed-killers.*

ANTHRACNOSE   Anthracnose is one of the less important rose diseases reported mostly on climbing roses and in regions where the winters are not severe. Small yellow, green or red spots that gradually become brown or purple with lighter-colored centers appear on the leaves and stems. As

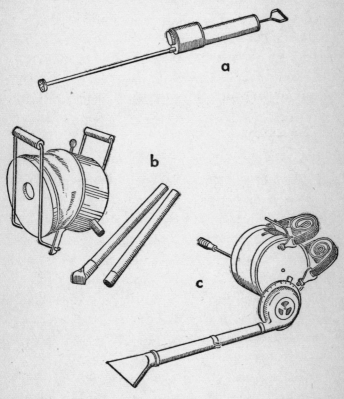

6. Dusters. *a) One-pound Hand Duster. b) Bellows Type Duster. Pressure is created by working the sides back and forth accordion fashion. c) Crank Duster. Turning the crank activates a fan which blows the dust out through the nozzle. Attachments are available for all three types for under-leaf dusting.*

the spots enlarge, injury occurs to the infected parts. Fungicides as suggested for black spot are effective controls. Spore germination requires four hours or more of moisture and distribution is not rapid.

APHIDS (PLANT LICE) These soft-bodied, green, pink or black, one-eighth-inch-long insects exist by sucking juices from new growth and blossom buds. Unless the infestation is particularly heavy, aphids probably cause more concern than actual damage. In extreme instances, they cause leaf curling, stunting and blossom deformity. Elimination is accomplished by one or more applications of sprays or dusts containing nicotine sulfate, rotenone or pyrethrum. Fresh tobacco dust or a spray consisting of 1½ teaspoonfuls of 40 per cent nicotine sulfate and one gallon of soapy water will give good results. To be effective, controls must contact the aphids and should, consequently, be directed to both surfaces of the leaves as well as to other infested portions of the plant.

BALLING OF BLOSSOMS If no disease or insect injury is apparent, this condition is probably caused by lack of potash in the soil, sudden temperature changes or insufficient root development.

BEETLES The Japanese beetle and the rose beetle are the most destructive members of this large group of chewing insects. The former attacks the buds, flowers and foliage of many plants; the latter definitely prefers the buds and partially opened flowers of the rose. Frequent applications, during periods of infestation, of a multi-purpose, DDT, chlordane or other spray or dust that has proven effective, will offer some control. Complete elimination, however, is difficult in any one particular garden as they arrive daily from adjoining gardens and fields. Destruction of the larvae in the soil during the pre-emergence period will greatly reduce the population during the forthcoming season. Your County Agent or State Agricultural College will tell you how this is best accomplished in your area.

The destruction of foliage by Japanese beetles during periods of extreme infestation will greatly reduce bloom production, and the few buds that are produced should be cut as they approach maturity and enjoyed indoors. Many rose growers remove all buds that appear during the peak of the beetle season and, in doing so, conserve the strength of the plant. This procedure usually results in more and better late summer and autumn bloom.

BLACK SPOT   The name of this widespread disease is distinctly appropriate as the initial symptoms are the appearance of small black, irregularly margined spots on the foliage. These spots later range in size from very small to the width of the leaf, and are frequently surrounded by a yellow halo. As the infection progresses, the leaves turn yellow and drop. Complete defoliation may occur if no preventative measures are taken.

Black spot is probably the most destructive of all rose diseases as it spreads rapidly and a nearly, or completely, defoliated plant cannot produce normal flowers or store the food required to insure winter survival.

Complete eradication during the current season is almost impossible after the disease has become established, but it may be restrained by the regular application of one of the several fungicides now available. These include sulfur, copper compounds, fermate, phygon and others. Some of these may injure the foliage if used during periods of extremely high temperatures, and others if wet, cool periods follow their application. The better multipurpose materials are reasonably safe when extreme conditions may be expected.

One ounce of fermate in 4 gallons of water, or 2 level teaspoons of fermate and 2 tablespoons of wettable sulfur in 1 gallon of water are suitable spray mixtures. One part fermate and 9 parts talc make an effective dust.

Continual vigilance is required as it is estimated that there may be as many as 30,000 black spot spores per quarter inch of leaf surface. These are distributed to other leaves by the splashing effect of water. Six hours of continuous moisture are sufficient for infection of leaves not covered with a protective fungicide. It is therefore apparent that artificial watering should not be done during the latter part of the day and spraying or dusting should be frequent.

Protection is particularly essential during periods of frequent rains or heavy dews.

Black spot may be delayed in the small garden by removing and burning the infected leaves as the disease becomes apparent, but this procedure does not obviate the necessity of applying a protective fungicide. Do not neglect to protect roses that are not seemingly affected, as few are entirely immune and the disease may be present although it may not have progressed sufficiently far to be apparent.

Infection may be minimized, or possibly prevented, by sprinkling the ground and the canes of the roses with a lime sulfur solution. This should be applied before growth begins in the spring and on a day when the temperature exceeds 40 degrees. If applied freely, the following formulas should kill any spores that have wintered in cane lesions or old leaves on the ground: One pound dry lime sulfur to 4 gallons of water, or, commercial liquid lime sulfur at the rate of 1 gallon to 8 gallons of water.

A mulch will serve as a mechanical barrier and, if applied early and thoroughly saturated with either of the above solutions, added protection will be provided. One pound of inexpensive lime sulfur is sufficient for at least fifty roses and can be applied, in solution, with a sprinkling can.

BORERS   Their presence is denoted by holes in the pith of pruned stems, on the sides of stems, or by a marked enlargement at point of injury. Weekly applications, during June and July, of beetle control insecticides will eliminate many of the insects responsible for borer infestation.

Pruning wounds should be painted or a thumb or carpet tack may be pressed into the pith. All infested stems should be removed and burned.

CANKERS   There are several different canker diseases but only two—brown and stem (or common) canker— are seriously destructive to the rose. Causes, ultimate effects and controls are practically the same for both, and neither is restricted to any particular region. Symptoms are the appearance of small, light brown, red, or purplish spots on the stems. These gradually enlarge and merge to form a large area of dead tissue, and when the stem has become completely girdled, the area above it will die.

In general, cankers appear chiefly in plants of low vitality or those on which the bark has suffered pruning, cultivating or winter injury. Crushed stems or stubs left by pruning too high above a bud are favored points of entry, and moisture-retaining mulches, in close contact with the stems, will increase the rapidity of development in these areas. When canker is discovered, the stem should be cut well below the infection and burned. The controls suggested for black spot (both summer and dormant) are usually effective after visibly diseased portions are removed.

CATERPILLARS   Few of these injure roses and those that do so may be controlled with multi-purpose sprays or dusts, or any of the stomach poison insecticides.

CHAFERS   The rose chafer is an awkward, long-legged, greenish tan-colored insect, about one-half inch in length; it is most abundant in areas where the soil is sandy, but is not confined to these areas. During the period of heaviest infestation—usually from mid-June to mid-July—they do considerable damage to the blossoms and foliage of many cultivated plants. Complete eradication is difficult as they are usually abundant and travel from garden to garden. Frequent applications of multi-purpose, DDT or pyrethrum dusts or sprays will minimize the damage. Hand picking is sometimes resorted to in areas of limited infestation.

CHLOROSIS (YELLOW LEAVES) Most prevalent in highly alkaline soils. For cause and remedy see *Purple Spots*.

CROWN GALL   The name is somewhat misleading as galls may develop on the roots or stems as well as on the crown. It is a bacterial disease occasionally introduced into the garden on new plants, or it may be present on land on which blackberries, raspberries, or other susceptible woody or herbaceous plants have been grown. State nursery inspections have greatly obviated the possibility of its being present on nursery-grown plants. Newly obtained roses, or other plants, having irregular, rough-textured, tumorlike growths should be rejected as there is no known cure. Amputation of the gall is not practical as the bacteria may be present on other portions of the plant and will contaminate the soil for at least two years following removal of the diseased plant.

If the disease develops on established plants, they should be burned and the soil with which the roots came in contact replaced with new soil. Crown-gall bacteria are rarely present in extremely acid soils, and the disease is more often a problem in the Southern states. Stunted, poor growth is a symptom, and although the plant may survive for several years, it does not justify the space it occupies.

DIE-BACK   Results from several causes, but is usually a secondary development of winter injury, deficiencies, excesses of food or water, or other diseases; it may be inherent. It is not a specific disease.

DROOPING, or WITHERED FLOWER STEMS   See *Balling*.

FAILURE TO PRODUCE LEAVES   When the stems remain green but no new growth is produced, the roots may have been partially destroyed by rodents or other causes. Restore plant balance by pruning top rather severely. Recently planted roses may have an air pocket under the roots or they may have become partially dried before planting. Either replant or soak the soil thoroughly.

GREEN-CENTERED BLOSSOMS May be characteristic of the variety, but sometimes results from frost injury to the buds.

HAIRY ROOT Characterized by the growth of a large mass of hairlike roots from any portion of the plant that has been in contact with the soil. Closely related to crown gall and precautionary measures are similar.

LEAF BURN Generally caused by improper use of sprays or dusts (follow manufacturers' recommendations) or the direct application to wet foliage of chemical fertilizers.

LEAF-CUTTER BEES Rarely sufficiently numerous to cause severe injury to the rose, although they attack it in two ways. They make a home for their young by drilling holes in the pith of unprotected, recently pruned, stems and cut circular pieces from rose leaves to feed them. For control see *Borers*.

LEAF HOPPER A small greenish yellow, wedge-shaped insect that jumps rapidly from leaf to leaf and causes injury similar to that of red-spider mite. They are rarely a serious problem and can be destroyed by dusting or spraying the lower surfaces of the leaves. DDT, nicotine, pyrethrum, rotenone or any of the multi-purpose materials are effective.

MIDGE This tiny yellow fly is responsible for many of the deformed buds and dead tips that are found on rose bushes. The damage results from destruction of the growing tissue by the maggots that hatch from the eggs deposited there by the adult form. Infested tips should be cut and burned and reinfestations discouraged by weekly applications of multi-purpose, DDT, lindane, or other insect-controlling dusts or sprays.

POWDERY MILDEW Especially prevalent on the West Coast and in the South, but may occur elsewhere when weather conditions are favorable. Development is encouraged by poor air circulation, high humidity and a succession of warm days and cool nights. Wet weather and temperatures above 85 degrees are unfavorable for germination of the freely produced spores which are wind-borne to adjacent plants and survive the winter mostly on persistent or fallen leaves. The disease is evidenced by a white, powderlike substance on young leaves, blossom buds and stems that frequently produces distortion and dwarfing of the infected part. Few roses are immune to mildew and the old type ramblers are particularly susceptible. Prevention should begin as soon as the first leaves develop as eradication is almost impossible when the weather is favorable and infection is established. Sulfur and copper compounds are effective controls.

PURPLE SPOTS (ON FOLIAGE) Usually results from nutritional deficiency and is evidence that the soil is lacking in some essential element. A soil analysis is suggested.

RODENT INJURY During the winter months, or when food is scarce, field mice will often chew the bark of roses that are in close proximity to their nests. Avoid using for winter mulching any material that is suitable for their nests (such as buckwheat hulls), or do not apply it until the ground is frozen and they have established homes elsewhere. Peat moss, cinders, shredded leaves, pine needles or ground corncobs are *not* suitable materials for nesting. A moth ball at the base of each plant is also a preventative. Pine mice are the most destructive of all rodents as they devour the roots, and their presence may remain unnoticed until the plants are seriously injured. Poison bait made by dissolving $\frac{1}{16}$ ounce powdered strychnine and the same amount of baking soda in $\frac{1}{3}$ cup of water and mixing with 1 quart of grain (corn, oats, rye or wheat) is effective. As this mixture is also fatal to birds and pets, it should be placed in exit holes and covered in such a manner that it can be reached only from below the surface.

ROOT KNOT   These small nodulelike swellings develop on the fibrous roots of roses and other plants. The disease is rarely a problem in the North as the nematodes that cause the swellings cannot survive low temperatures. Stunted growth and premature death are the ultimate results. Where the trouble is prevalent, your County Agent or State Experimental Station will suggest soil treatment. Precautionary measures as prescribed for crown gall should be followed.

ROSE-STEM GALLS   These should not be confused with crown galls as they are caused by wasplike insects rather than bacteria. The insects deposit their eggs in the stems and the resultant larvae cause the stems to swell and produce a gall-like growth. These assume various forms and may appear on any above-ground portion of the stem. They are not fatal to the plant, but should be removed so as to destroy the larvae. This is the only known preventative.

RUST   Common leaf rust is prevalent in regions having cool, humid summers and mild winters and is rarely serious elsewhere. It is characterized by the appearance of small, deep orange-colored spots on the foliage. These spots invariably have a narrow green or brown border, and as the season advances, become almost black. Defoliation is rapid and serious, particularly in the Pacific Coast states. The spores responsible for spring infection winter in the tissues of fallen leaves, and the preventative measures as well as the controls prescribed for black spot are effective.

SCALE INSECTS   Widely distributed but rarely a serious problem. Stems heavily infested with these tiny white sucking insects should be removed and burned. The others should be sprayed, when dormant, with 1 part commercial lime-sulfur in 9 parts water, or, $\frac{1}{2}$ cup of white-oil emulsion concentrate in 1 gallon of water. The latter formula is preferred near painted surfaces. During the growing season, the spray should consist of $1\frac{1}{2}$ teaspoons of nicotine sulphate in 1 gallon of soapy water. Controls suggested for aphids are also usually effective.

SLUGS   Rarely a serious problem although the resultant skeletonized leaves are rather unsightly. Most dusts or sprays will destroy these dark green larvae of the sawfly.

SPIDER MITES   Probably one of the most serious enemies of the rose as they multiply rapidly and are difficult to detect before they have caused considerable foliage injury. They are minute (less than $\frac{1}{50}$ of an inch long), oval, eight-legged pests and may be either greenish yellow, dark red, or spotted. Leaves attacked have a stippled gray-

ish appearance and soon become brown and fall. Control
is a problem as they live mostly in dense colonies on the
undersurface of the leaf where they spin their webs and
exist by sucking leaf juices. Many of the most effective
controls are toxic to humans and should be used with caution. Fortunately, the mites can exist only under hot, dry
conditions and a spray of water directed at the underside
of the leaves in early morning will give fair results. Dusting sulfur or dust containing 1 per cent rotenone are also
moderately effective. When the infestation is particularly
heavy, more drastic measures should be taken, and ara-
mite, dimite, or malathon sprays, diluted as recommended
by the manufacturer, are suggested. If the first application does not give satisfactory control, it should be re-
peated a week later. This is usually necessary.

STEM GIRDLER   See *Borers*.

THRIPS   Roses are not the favorite food plants of these
tiny active yellow or brown insects, but they do cause extensive injury to roses during periods of hot, dry weather
and particularly to those that produce light-colored flowers. Thrips are often responsible for spotted, discolored or
deformed flowers, and when injury to the buds is extensive,
they may fail to open. Either of the foregoing symptoms
offers evidence that they are present and conclusive proof
can be obtained by shaking a blossom that is thought to be
infested over a sheet of white paper. Eradication is difficult as they exist on portions of the bud that are largely
inaccessible to dusts or sprays. However, they are continually migrating from one blossom to another and, if the
developing buds are kept coated with multi-purpose, DDT,

rotenone, pyrethrum, lindane, or nicotine sprays or dusts, many are destroyed. Probably more effective is the removal and burning of all infested buds and blossoms during the period when the infestation is heaviest.

Whether dust or spray is preferred—many growers use both—good equipment is essential (Figs. 5 and 6). The number of plants to be treated will govern the size used.

In conclusion, *use sprays and dusts only as recommended by the manufacturer*. They are safe if properly handled, but may prove harmful to humans as well as pets and plants if they are not.

chapter seven

Pruning

The beginner is often reluctant to attempt pruning as he is fearful that, due to lack of experience, he may seriously injure his plants.

Actually, there is nothing complicated, mysterious or technical about pruning roses, and in no phase of rose growing is greater leeway permitted. Experienced growers still disagree as to whether a plant should be pruned severely, moderately or lightly, and they present rather convincing arguments in favor of their preferred method. These conflicting recommendations naturally confuse the beginner, and he would probably be just as successful and enjoy the task more if he used his own initiative. He should, however, know why pruning is desirable, the fundamentals of procedure and a few facts concerning plant life. The balance of this chapter should supply the required information.

Pruning accomplishes several purposes; it improves the

appearance, health and productiveness of the plant by replacing old wood with new, better adapts it to the place where it is grown, causes it to be less susceptible to disease, stimulates good growth, and improves the quality of the flowers.

If we examine a forest tree or a wildling shrub, we discover that Nature prunes by destroying branches that are weak or have outlived their usefulness. Nature, however, is interested primarily in efficiency rather than beauty; and corrective pruning in the garden must be somewhat more drastic if the plant is to attain its full beauty.

The preliminary steps, applicable to all types of roses, consist of (1) the removal of all dead wood, (2) the cutting out of all weak, useless, or diseased growth, and (3) the shaping of the plant. In some instances, these three steps will suffice, but it is often necessary, or at least desirable, to shorten the retained growth so as to improve blossom production. The rose family is comprised of widely diversified types and as specific pruning requirements differ somewhat, they are discussed separately.

There are some pruning fundamentals, however, that apply to all roses as well as to other shrubs. The pruning shears should be sharp and held so that the cutting, or thin, blade is toward the part of the stem you wish to retain. The cut should be made not more than $1/4$ inch above a bud and as much strong, healthy wood as possible should be retained (Fig. 7).

The leaves and roots are the food-gathering equipment of the plant and as they work in unison, it is obvious that the unnecessary removal, or severe cutting back, of young

healthy canes will retard growth and reduce blossom production. Extremely old canes, however, are comparatively
unproductive and should be occasionally replaced with
new ones. Gradual renewal is accomplished by cutting out
about ⅓ of the older canes each year.

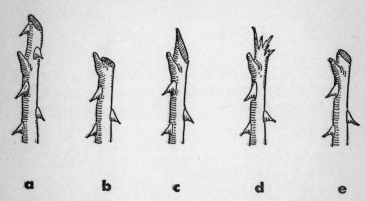

a   b   c   d   e

7. Pruning. *a) Too far above bud. b) Too close to bud. c) Cut
at wrong angle. d) Ragged; torn, not cut. e) Correct angle
and position.*

When an exceptionally vigorous shoot appears, its
source should be investigated. If it grew from below the
crown of the plant, it is a sucker, or wild shoot, and should
be torn out at the socket. Cutting back will not eliminate it
and, if permitted to grow, the portion of the plant above
will gradually die of starvation. The foliage and thorns of
a wild shoot are different than those of the rest of the
plant, but this alone is an uncertain means of identifica-
tion, as new growth frequently has an entirely different appearance than old. None of the roses used as rootstocks
are desirable inhabitants of the rose bed as they are too
vigorous and the blossoms are comparatively inferior.

The spring pruning of varieties that are not dependably winter hardy occasionally presents a problem. Externally, a cane may appear to be uninjured although the internal portions have suffered injury that will cause its early death. Winter injury is denoted by the color of the pith, which is normally white. If it is brown, the cane should be gradually cut back until healthy pith is reached, Canes that are larger in diameter than a pencil should have their cut ends protected so as to prevent the entry of borers. A dab of tree paint, shellac or chewing gum will serve the purpose, although it is usually easier to push a small carpet or thumb tack into the cut end.

The major pruning of all roses, except the ramblers, should be performed during their dormant season. The most suitable time is just before spring growth begins as winter injury can be determined and the cuts heal more rapidly.

Pruning, as it applies specifically to each group, is discussed in the following paragraphs.

Hybrid tea, tea and hybrid perpetuals

The region in which the grower lives is usually the controlling factor in pruning roses of this group. Where winter injury is severe, he has no alternative but to cut back to live wood, but in others, he may practice severe, moderate or tall pruning. A severely pruned plant (3 to 5 inches from the crown) will usually produce the best individual blooms, but they will be few in number. Moderate pruning (12 to 18 inches) will induce fair production of good quality flowers, and a plant that has been pruned but lightly, or not at all, will bear many comparatively small blossoms.

The advocates of minimum pruning are increasing in number as they have found that even an unpruned plant will produce high-quality blossoms if a few of the buds are removed as soon as they become visible. Flower production is in proportion to the leaf area and approximately 6 healthy leaves are required to manufacture sufficient food to produce an average bloom. It is therefore apparent that a large plant will produce considerably more buds than a small one, and that the size of the individual blossom may be increased by eliminating some of the buds.

Pruning, however, should not be entirely neglected as wood ceases to be fully productive after 3 or 4 years, and the growth may become too crowded. It is advisable to remove a few of the older canes each year.

The cutting of roses for the home constitutes a minor pruning operation. If cut with short stems, the plant will benefit, but cutting long stems decreases later production. Whenever feasible, the stems should be cut just above the first five-foliate leaf (Fig. 9a). Spent blooms should also be removed at the same point.

Disbudding is often practiced by those who prefer one exceptionally fine bloom to two or more of average quality. It is accomplished by removing all but the center bud at an early stage of development. The food is thus diverted to the one bud (Fig 9b).

Polyanthas, floribundas and Chinas

As the value of these roses depends mostly on the mass of bloom rather than on the quality of the individual blossoms, the pruning should be limited to the removal of dead, old, or diseased branches and the shaping of the plants.

Old-fashioned, species and shrub roses

Pruning should be confined to the cutting out of dead and very old wood and the shaping of the plant. The grace and beauty of many of these roses will be destroyed if they are pruned too severely.

Creeping roses

Remove only the dead wood.

Climbing roses

The large-flowered climbers such as *Blaze* and *New Dawn* bloom on new wood that grows from the older canes and pruning should be limited to the removal of unwanted growth. A gradual renewal of the plant can be effected by cutting out one or two of the older canes each year. Bloom production will be more evenly distributed if the lateral branches are cut back to 4 or 6 buds. Repeat bloom is encouraged on some varieties by removing faded blooms.

Rambler roses

These are best pruned immediately after flowering as they produce blossoms mostly on new wood. The removal of old canes at their base encourages the growth of new and vigorous shoots.

Pillar roses

Unless winter injury occurs, they require pruning only to keep them within bounds. As many varieties of this group produce the best blossoms on wood that is 2 or 3 years old, adequate winter protection is more important than pruning.

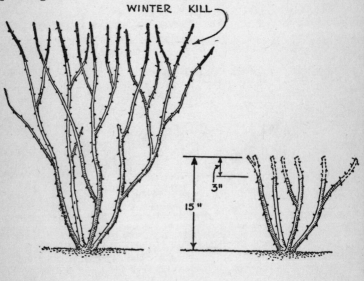

WINTER KILL

3"

15 "

a   b

8. Cutting Back Winter Kill. *a) Before. b) After.*

PRUNING   Fig. 7 shows some of the commonest errors
made in pruning, and the one proper way to cut.

Where winter kill occurs hybrid tea, tea and hybrid perpetuals must be cut back to the live wood even though only

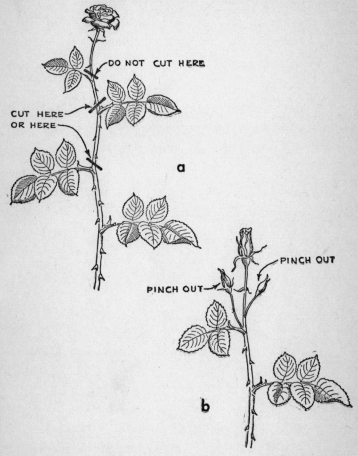

9. **Pruning for Additional Bloom.** *a) Cutting at five foliated leaf.
b) Disbudding to permit center bud to benefit. To disbud
for exhibition, the stems of side buds should be torn or
cut out at base.*

a few inches of stem remain. A healthy, sturdy plant may be pruned back to from twelve to eighteen inches from the ground (Fig. 8).

The cutting of buds and fully developed or withered blossoms is, to a certain degree, pruning for additional bloom. Always cut back to a five foliated leaf (Plate 9a). Fewer but larger flowers can be obtained by disbudding (Plate 9b).

chapter eight

Winter protection

A vast majority of our most popular roses are not hardy and require winter protection in many parts of this country. Casualties may be prevented, or at least reduced, if the factors causing them are known and suitable preventative measures are taken.

Late-season growth should be discouraged as it will rarely survive the winter and depletes the food reserve of the plant. It is induced by fertilization, watering, heavy pruning and cultivation later than two months before the normal dormant season.

A rose bush, like a hibernating animal, must prepare during the late summer for a long winter sleep. As the leaves are the food-making agents of the plant, as many as possible should be maintained in a healthy condition. This is best accomplished by cutting flowers with short stems and following a regular dusting or spraying program.

The importance of a well-drained bed has already been mentioned, but deserves repeating as few roses will survive the winter in water-logged soil.

Atmospheric conditions greatly influence the effect of cold. A cold spell of long duration will cause more injury than a brief one and continuous cold winds from the same direction are more harmful than "still" cold. Winter sun following a cold night is also responsible for considerable damage as it causes rapid and extensive temperature fluctuations and this results in injury to the plant cells. The sudden, and often unexpected, arrival of extremely low temperatures before the wood is sufficiently hardened is a contributing factor to winter casualties.

Snow covering is also important as a variety not adapted to regions of normally light snowfall might winter satisfactorily in a colder climate where heavy snows cover it throughout the coldest periods.

It is therefore not safe to assume that the hardiness of a variety is to be determined only by the mean temperature of the region in which it is grown. If the plant is healthy and other conditions are to its liking, the wood of the average hybrid tea suffers no injury at temperatures of 5 degrees above zero, the floribundas at zero, and the polyanthas at 5 degrees below. The climbers differ considerably in their resistance, but most of the so-called "hardy" types can withstand zero or slightly below.

To prevent the possibility of injury from a sudden severe drop in temperature and to avoid the necessity of working during cold weather, protection may be applied early in the fall. More plants are lost through delayed protection than by premature protection. In regions similar to that of northern Ohio, the end of October is usually an ideal time to accomplish this task. Mid-October is more suitable in colder regions. However, the extremely long canes, which would whip around during the winter and be dead by spring, should not be cut back until the foliage has fallen.

Practically all the bedding roses that require protection can be wintered successfully by applying an 8- to 12-inch mound of soil over the plant in the manner used to protect the newly planted. More wood will be retained by building the higher mound and, if there is sufficient ambition, it may exceed 12 inches. When roses are planted farther than 18 inches apart, the required soil may be drawn up from between the plants, but the roots should not be exposed. Otherwise, it must be hauled in. Additional protection, though usually unnecessary, may be afforded by placing well-rotted manure or other soil-shading material over the mounds but not in direct contact with the plant.

The mounds should be removed as soon as the possibility of temperatures below 15 degrees are past. Tender new growth may be injured by late uncovering while that which develops after uncovering hardens gradually and will withstand late spring freezes. Early uncovering also permits the application of dormant sprays before growth begins.

Climbing roses requiring protection should be laid on the ground and completely covered with soil where the winters are severe. In more moderate regions, they may be left on the supports, or laid on the ground and wrapped in water repellent, non-transparent paper or other material. Freezing nights, sunshiny days and high winds wreak the greatest havoc with climbers.

The winter protection of tree roses presents a problem. Various methods have been tried, but in severe climates, best results are obtained by loosening the roots on one side, bending the entire plant to the ground and covering it completely with soil. Where the winters are only moderately severe, the plant may remain in the ground if straw, excelsior or a similar material is packed between and around the branches. Waterproof paper should then be wrapped and securely tied around the entire mass. Bracing to prevent wind damage is vitally important.

Winter injury is often not apparent until late spring as external evidence is frequently lacking. The stem may begin to produce normal foliage and blossoms, but will suddenly die as the damaged internal parts are unable to supply the increased demand for food and water. Brown pith usually denotes injury.

chapter nine

Allied hobbies

The enjoyment that may be derived from roses is not confined entirely to their culture, and the enthusiast will invariably become interested in one or more of several allied pursuits. They afford an opportunity to satisfy artistic, creative or scientific impulses and add greatly to the pleasures of rose growing.

Several centuries ago, our ancestors discovered that the rose possessed more than floral beauty and used the fruits and/or blossoms in making medicines, sachets and jewelry, and in cooking. As recently as World War II, European countries collected rose fruits for their vitamin-C content, but the other ancient usages are now rarely practiced.

The modern rose hobbyist has adopted more modern pastimes such as rose breeding, propagating, exhibiting, photography, flower arranging, and collecting varieties of bygone days.

Any of these offer almost unlimited possibilities in adding zest to rose growing and may be entered into as lightly or seriously as desired.

Plant breeding

The word "hybridizing" has been very aptly defined as "a fascinating game of chance between man and plants." This is particularly true when garden roses are the subjects as their ancestry is so complex that results cannot be predicted by any mathematical rule. If they could be, rose breeding would lose much of its interest. The amateur hybridist, however, should have a definite objective, and use, as parents, varieties that possess the characteristics he hopes to combine in the progeny. A perfect combination may not result, but it is possible, and he will have a lot of fun trying to effect it.

Some roses transmit their characteristics better than others, and some (particularly in the floribunda class) are sterile and therefore incapable of producing seed. The following are exceptionally good seed parents:

Blanche Mallerin	*McGredy's Ivory*
Carrousel	*Mrs. Paul R. Bosley*
Donald Prior	*Nocturne*
Edith Krause	*Red Pinnochio*
First Love	*Soeur Therese*
Masquerade	*Velvetier*

World's Fair

The first step in hybridizing (Fig. 10) is to select a bud that should open within the next twenty-four hours and, with

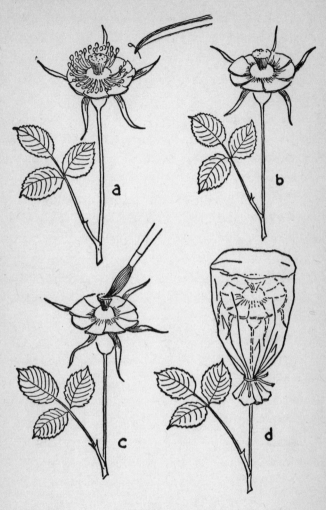

10. Hybridizing. *a) Removing sepals, petals and stamens.
b) Calyx, styles and stigmas remaining. c) Pollinating with
camel's hair brush. d) Paper cover to prevent entrance
of unwanted pollen.*

the aid of a pair of tweezers, remove all the sepals, petals and stamens (the male organs). This operation is referred to as "emasculating." The flower parts that remain are the calyx, styles and stigmas. The calyx surrounds the ovary in which the seeds develop and later becomes the fruit, or hip. Soon after the pollen is applied to the stigmas, a microscopic tube descends, through the style, to the ovary where it fertilizes the egg. This is the nucleus of the seed.

When the stigmas are ready to accept pollen, they become slightly enlarged and have a sticky appearance. This usually occurs about the time that the blossom would have normally opened.

At the time of emasculation, select an almost-open bud of the variety you intend to use as the male, or pollen, parent. Remove the sepals and petals and cut stem to about one inch. Then place it, on a small dish, in a warm room, until the yellow pollen grains are visible. When this occurs, the "pollen brush" is ready to be dabbed gently onto the stigmas. After you have completed this operation, attach a tag to the stem of the pollinated flower and write on it the name of the pollen parent. From the time the bud is emasculated until a day or two after pollenizing, it should be kept covered with a small paper bag or envelope. This will prevent the entrance of unwanted pollen.

Complete seed development usually requires about 3 months and, when it is accomplished, the fruits become yellow, orange, or red tinted, and may be harvested. Remove the seeds from the fruits and plant them immediately (about $3/16$ inch deep) in a flat or pot. A mixture of equal parts of soil, sand and peat moss provides a good germinating medium as it remains loose and friable for a long time.

After the seeds have been planted and the soil moistened, the containers should be placed in the basement, or other cool spot, until the first seedlings appear. The time required is uncertain. Germination may begin within a month and continue throughout the winter, slow down or stop during the summer, and start again with the arrival of cool weather. The soil should be kept moist at all times.

It is advisable to plant the seedlings in individual pots as soon as they are large enough to handle. Higher temperatures are required for growth than for germination. When weather permits, the seedlings should be planted outdoors.

It's a thrill to watch the first blossoms develop on a seedling of your own origination, and many of the roses that beautify our gardens are the result of the efforts of the amateur breeder.

Propagation

The desire to grow a rose that is unobtainable, commercially, occurs quite frequently. It may be an admired variety in a friend's garden or one that possesses sentimental value. There are three possible ways of satisfying the desire. You might induce the owner to layer a branch, obtain a cutting and root it under a fruit jar, or, try the more intricate process of budding.

Layering is probably the easiest and surest method. Simply select a branch that may be bent so that a portion of it (not the tip) may be covered with soil. Roots will eventually develop where the branch is covered, and when they are sufficiently numerous, the new plant may be separated from the parent. Rooting will occur more readily if the covered portion is cut or broken slightly and the soil is kept moist. A stone or brick placed over the soil will help to retain moisture and hold the branch in place.

Cuttings, or slips, provide an easy method of propagation and are successful with most roses. Those taken after the foliage has fallen in late autumn, but before the wood has frozen, are referred to as hardwood or dormant cuttings. Medium-sized stems of the preceding summer's growth are cut into 6- to 8-inch lengths with a dormant bud about $\frac{1}{8}$ inch from each end. They are then packed in sand, sawdust, or other moisture-retaining material, and stored in a cool, but not freezing, location over winter. The cuttings should be planted outdoors as early in the spring as possible with about $\frac{3}{4}$ of their length below the surface, and with the buds pointing upward. Their subsequent handling is similar to that prescribed for softwood cuttings.

The latter are 5- to 6-inch lengths of flowering shoots with all but the upper leaf removed. The lower cut is made just below a bud and they are planted 3 to 4 inches deep in loose soil or sand and covered with a fruit jar. When new shoots appear (in 5 or 6 weeks), the jar should be tilted slightly so as to permit the entrance of more air, and a week or two later, it may be removed. Shade and ample moisture must be provided during the period of rooting.

Commercial growers propagate by budding as a larger

and better plant can be produced in less time by this method (Fig. 11). The procedure is somewhat complicated, but is not difficult. Suitable understocks (the root system) may be purchased or produced from cuttings or seeds. R. multiflora is best adapted to the purpose as it is easy to propagate and grows rapidly.

As the bud is inserted on the main stem between the roots and lowest branch, they should be at least 1 inch apart. It is frequently necessary to clear the required space by removing a branch or two before planting the understock. Plant so that the area where bud is to be inserted is just above the ground level and cover it with soil. This prevents the bark from becoming too hard and woody to peel readily. In fact, the ease with which the bark separates from the wood is the factor that determines the time of budding. In most regions, this is usually during July, August and September. If the weather is extremely dry, it may be necessary to soak the soil a few days before.

Now for the actual mechanics of budding. Select a plant whose main stem is about ⅜ inch in diameter and make a horizontal cut (with the tip of a sharp knife) about ¼ inch long just under the lowest branch and from the center of this cut, make a downward cut of about 1 inch. The result is a cut in the form of a letter "T" that extends through the bark *but not into the wood*. Then place the point of the blade at the intersection of the two cuts and gently pull back the bark on both sides of the vertical cut so as to expose the cambium layer. If it separates easily, the stock is in good condition and the bark may be pressed back (to prevent drying out) until the bud shield is ready.

The best buds are found about midway on a shoot that has just finished blooming. Examine those at the base of each leaf stem and select one that is mature and plump. Place the blade of the knife about 1 inch above the bud and make a slicing downward cut under the bud and to about ½ inch below it. The piece cut out is called the *bud shield*. A better union will result if the wood behind the bud is removed, and this may usually be accomplished by pinching the shield very lightly between the thumb and forefinger. Under no circumstances should the bud be crushed or the heart torn out. This is the most difficult and exacting of all budding operations and the beginner should practice it on buds that are not valuable.

The bud shield is inserted beneath the bark of the understock incision by placing the lower point at the intersection of the two cuts and forcing it downward until it reaches the bottom of the vertical cut. If a small portion of the leaf stem was left on the shield, it will serve as a handle. Cut off cleanly any bark that projects above the "T." The shield is then "tied in" by wrapping with a cut rubber band. Begin wrapping at the bottom by making the first lap over the end of the band and gradually work upwards. Overlapping is not necessary, but the entire incision, with the exception of the bud, should be covered. Another half hitch at the top will hold the wrapping in place.

About 3 weeks later, the wrapping should be cut and the bud examined. If it is still green, your efforts have been successful. If not, another bud may be inserted on the opposite side. In most instances, the bud will remain dormant until the following spring, but, in either event, it requires protection where winters are severe. The following spring, the top of the rootstock should be cut back to

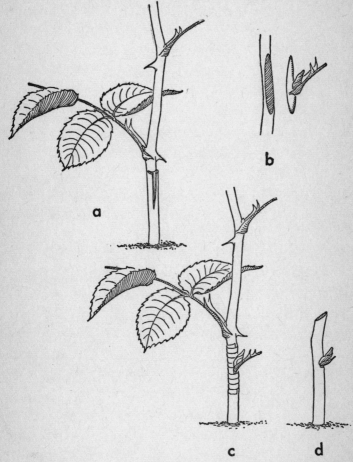

11. Budding. *a) Understock prepared for bud. b) Bud shield cut away. c) Bud in place on understock and wrapped with rubber band. d) Understock cut to within one inch of bud just before growth begins the following spring.*

about 1 inch above the bud. All shoots emanating from the bud require tying to a stake as they grow rapidly and the union is rarely sufficiently strong to support them until midsummer. If they are cut back slightly, they are less liable to wind injury and more canes will be produced from the bud.

Exhibiting

Exhibiting your roses in the local flower show or county fair is a lot of fun. You may not win a blue ribbon on your first attempt, but by observing the entries of those who did, you will probably learn why. Proper timing is important as the blooms should be from half to two thirds open when judged, and the variety, handling, and the temperature of the show room and container water are factors that influence opening. General advice to the novice is to cut blooms in late afternoon, remove spray residue from foliage, plunge stems into cold water almost to base of bloom, and place in a dark, cool, draftless room overnight (or wrap carefully in waxed paper and place in the refrigerator). They may be transported to the show either in the container or in waxed paper with damp newspaper wrapped around the base of the stems. Every precaution should be taken to prevent injury to the petals and foliage. Spent blooms should be removed from cluster-flowered varieties and side buds from those that bloom individually.

The scale of points usually used in judging are Form (25), Substance (20), Color (25), Stem and Foliage (20) and Size (10). These are defined as follows:

Form—A pointed or high-centered rose is best for show purposes. One having faulty shape, irregular petalage or a split center is usually disqualified.

Substance—Petals should be firm, not soft.

Color—Fresh and typical of the variety.

Stem and foliage—The best stems are straight and in proportion to the size of the bloom. Foliage clean and undamaged by insects or handling.

Size—This is relative to the size normally produced by the variety.

A few tips on raising prize-winning roses. Water frequently as water will produce larger blooms, add substance to the petals, give stronger stems and improve the color of the blooms and foliage. Feed, and spray or dust regularly. About 3 weeks before the show select the buds that you believe will be at the proper stage of development at show time. Then remove all side buds from the stem so that all the energy will be diverted into the center bud. The selection of buds is a gamble as weather conditions control the speed of development. The best procedure is to disbud all stems 3 weeks before the show. They may miss the show, but you will have better and larger blooms for the home.

Roses in the home

Roses are desirable subjects for home decoration as they may be used in a variety of ways and are appropriate to every occasion. A single bloom, in a suitable vase, will create a friendly atmosphere in a room or at the office and one on the breakfast table will start the day on a cheerful note.

Other flowers, particularly those of a "spiky" nature, such as snapdragons, miniature gladioluses and delphiniums, may be used to advantage with roses in arrangements.

The subject of flower arranging is too intricate to discuss fully in this chapter, but if the novice knows a few of the basic fundamentals, the result should be satisfying and restful. Roses are attractive regardless of how they are arranged, but their beauty may be further enhanced by placing them properly in a rather conservative vase or container. An ornate one detracts from the blossoms and gives the arrangement a "confused" appearance.

One of the most important factors in successful rose arranging is seasoning the blooms so that they will remain fresh for the longest possible time. This is accomplished by cutting in late afternoon and placing them immediately, and overnight, in cold water. Warm air and drafts will hasten deterioration. A rose with many petals will usually last longer than one with a few petals. Do not cut with longer stems than necessary, as this is detrimental to the plant.

The first step is to visualize where the flowers are to be placed and consider the container, flowers and foliage in relation to the color and size of the background. All should harmonize in color and texture. The next is to select a container and place pin flower holders or chicken wire in the bottom of it so that the arrangement will be stabilized. The flower holders may be fastened securely to the container by placing floral, or modeling, clay between them (when they are dry) and by pressing them down firmly with a twisting motion.

The placement of flowers and foliage is best accomplished in four operations. The tallest stems should be placed first and the portion above the rim of the container should be at least 1½ times that of the height of a vertical container or the greatest dimension of a horizontal one. The second placement should be half as tall as the first, and the third, half that of the second. The arrangement may now be "softened" by adding other stems of various heights.

Large foliage and darker-colored blossoms placed where the stems converge, give visual stability to the design.

Buds, small or light-colored blossoms and spiky material should be placed on the outside of the design, and the larger and deeper-colored flowers on the inside. This attracts attention to the center of the arrangement which is the focal, or major, point.

Roses of almost any color may be placed in white, gray or black containers as they are neutral colors.

By following the preceding suggestions, you attain good proportion, balance, focus and unity, and the finished arrangement should present a pleasing picture.

Searching for old roses

Many people have found that the search for old roses is a hobby in which the entire family can find enjoyment and in which all can partake. Old homesteads, cemeteries and mining camps throughout the country are fertile hunting grounds, and a surprisingly large number of different varieties can be found in them.

As they grow lustily and many of them sucker freely, the owners, or custodians, as the case may be, are usually glad to give a "start" to anyone who is sufficiently interested to ask for it. It is regrettable that some few individuals permit their enthusiasm to overcome their better judgment and do not obtain permission before digging or cutting.

The survival of so many of these pioneer roses attests to their vitality and value. Someone admired them sufficiently to grow and tend them even when fashion had declared new favorites. They are rugged individuals that give much and demand little. It is true that they bloom but once each year, but the annual display is so grand and glorious, and the fragrance so enchanting, that they are endeared to all who know them.

Definitely out of place in a bed with the modern roses, they are ideal in the border or background where they might very well replace spirea, mock orange, forsythia and allied shrubs.

Hobbies add much to the enjoyment of living, and in collecting old roses, we may enjoy a hobby that is educational, exceedingly interesting and comparatively inexpensive. The old roses, besides being things of beauty, are easy to grow and form a living link between the past and the present.

7960

RINEHART'S GARDEN LIBRARY

(continued from front end paper)

that when I disappeared she could always find me in the garden eating green peas or admiring a rose. I still like both." I can't vouch for the peas, but the American Rose Society and the thousands of visitors who flock annually to his gardens at Medina, Ohio, to see the more than 3500 varieties under cultivation will gladly testify to the fact that Mr.